YOU CAN'T AFFORD TO GET HACKED

The must-have practical guide to keeping your household safe online

AMJAD PIROTTI & AMIR ROKNIFARD

Copyright © 2020

Amjad Pirotti & Amir Roknifard

All rights reserved. No part of this work may be reproduced or stored in an information retrieval system (other than for purposes of review) without the express permission of the publisher in writing.

CONTENTS

Why Should You Understand Cybersecurity? 1
    What Is The Internet? 2
    The Dark Side of The Internet 3
    A Cyber-Attack Can Change Everything 5
    It's Easy to Assume You're Not At Risk 6
    Cybersecurity Is Complicated Though, Isn't It? 10

Your Cybersecurity In Public 13
    What Is A Public Network? 14
    What Is A Public Station? 15
    What Is Public Wi-Fi? 15
    What Are The Risks? 16
    How to Stay Safe on Public Wi-Fi 22
    What If You Suspect You've Been Hacked? 24
    Protect Yourself As Well As You Can 25

Securing Your Personal Information At Home 27
    Shopping and Banking Online 27
    Protecting Your Passwords 31
    Using Antivirus 34
    Maintaining Good Email Security 36
    Using Usbs 38
    Some Additional Things To Remember 40
    Phone Security 42

    Nothing Is Free on The Internet 45

    Smart Home 47

Don't Give Away More Than You Mean to on Social Media 53

    What's The Danger? 54

    What Goes Online, Stays Online 55

    Oversharing And Identity Theft 56

    Your Online Accounts Are All Connected 57

    How Can You Protect Yourself? 59

    Tips for Securing Your Social Media 61

    Social Media Can Be Great 63

Scam Alert! Do Not Be The Victim Of A Fraud! 65

    Social Engineering 65

    In An Email 66

    In A Phone Call 74

    In A Text 75

    In An Exciting Offer or Opportunity 77

    On Social Media 78

    Don't Fall For Their Tricks! 79

    Some Final Thoughts 83

Tech-Savvy Kids 85

    Cyberbullying 87

    Sexual Predators 89

    Pornography 91

    Additional Technical Control Measures 92

Social Media	95
YouTube Kids	100
Additional Advice	103
Now You're Ready!	106

Why Should You Understand Cybersecurity?

The internet has had an enormous impact on how we live our lives. It has changed the way we shop, the way we work, the way we learn, the way we communicate with each other.

We spend, on average, almost seven hours of each day online[1]. That's a huge amount of time! Whether you want to order some food, wish a friend a happy birthday, find out what people thought of a new movie or get directions to the airport, the internet is there to help you.

Without the internet, society as we know it would come grinding to a halt, and we're not here to argue that there's anything wrong with that! But the internet isn't purely a force for good, so while you're enjoying it freely, it's also important to know how to protect yourself and your family. That's where this book comes in.

---

[1] 6 hours and 42 minutes per day, according to the Digital 2019 report by Hootsuite and We Are Social.

What Is The Internet?

That might seem like an obvious question, but what is it, really? Using the internet, we can accomplish truly amazing things. We can send ideas and information from one end of the world to the other within seconds. We can live out whole alternative lives in online game worlds, shared with communities of people scattered across the planet. The internet is full of ways to share our lives with others, through photos and videos, text and sound.

We can do all of this easily, and with confidence, without needing to have any understanding of what makes it all possible. In many ways, this is a great thing! You don't need to understand the internet to share an important personal story with people all over the world. You don't need to understand the internet to donate money to a cause you believe in, or to take online courses that will enhance your life and help you to earn more money.

The internet, essentially, is a network. It's connections. And while it can be the most amazing tool, those connections can also be taken advantage of.

In the same way that you can go to Wikipedia and search for some information about a celebrity you find interesting, there are people who can find and use the information you've put online about yourself. This is the danger of the internet.

The Dark Side of the Internet

There is an increasing awareness of the privacy issues that arise when living your life online, and a growing understanding that the internet isn't as safe as it might appear. A number of high-profile events involving the hacking of cloud storage, or stolen passwords, have forced people to face up to the fact that their online information isn't always as secure as they would like it to be.

Social media is enormously popular, and many people have accounts across a range of sites, but there have been legitimate privacy concerns raised about these platforms. Everything you do online leaves a trail, and the way you use social media gives companies a lot of information about you; your location, your interests, your likes and your dislikes. Companies can also easily get hold of other personal information, such as your email address and phone number, your home address, where you work and where you spend your money. Hackers will work hard to obtain this kind of information in order to sell it on. And it's not just hackers you need to be aware of when it comes to social media.

Did you know?

75% of attacks on social media are carried out by "bots" - programs written by hackers to automate hacking attempts - according to a study by Arkose Labs.

If a bot can gain access to an account, it can get access to all of that account's personal information, and sell it to the highest bidder.

You Can't Afford to Get Hacked

It's your information, and you should have the right to complete control over it, but the social media platforms aren't always transparent about what they do with it once it's in their hands. This kind of data can be worth a lot of money to advertisers, and users aren't necessarily asked for permission before their information is sold off.

The US Federal Trade Commission investigated Facebook in 2018 over concerns that users' personal information was being illegally obtained and sold on to third parties.

There have been a number of significant data breaches, threatening the personal (and sometimes financial) information of millions of people. In 2017 Equifax, one of the largest credit bureaus in the US, confessed there had been a data breach compromising the personal information of 143 million consumers.

In 2018, 16 sites, including MyFitnessPal and Dubsmash, were compromised, and the passwords of an estimated 150 million customers were stolen and put up for sale. In 2019 Zynga (the game developer behind Farmville) was hacked. The hacker had access to 218 million registered accounts, and email addresses, passwords, user IDs and phone numbers were stolen.

Those are just a few examples of real, significant data breaches from the last few years. There have been many more than this, and there will be more in the future. As fast as companies learn, hackers and cyber-criminals are always working to find ways to steal information.

Why Should You Understand Cybersecurity

A Cyber-Attack Can Change Everything

Although it's easy to assume that none of these things will happen to you, the fact is online security is critical, and everyone needs to be aware of it. With the rise of COVID-19 and the necessity of social distancing, more people than ever are turning to the internet.

It's helping us to feel connected to friends we can't see right now, it's allowing workers to continue doing their jobs from the safety of their homes, and it's keeping everybody entertained without the need to go outside. Unfortunately, this also means it's a great opportunity for cyber-criminals.

There are a number of ways that some people are trying to take advantage of the current pandemic, such as the use of phishing emails, apps, websites or files that look like they provide useful information or advice on COVID-19. When accessed though, these can infect your device with malware or ransomware, causing problems that take a lot of time or money to fix. That is, if they're fixable at all.

> **Did you know?**
>
> "Phishing" is the practice of sending fraudulent emails that pretend to be from a trusted source - such as your bank, or an online service you've signed up for - in order to trick people into sending personal information.
>
> Phishing is the cause of 90% of data breaches, according to retruster.

You Can't Afford to Get Hacked

There are a number of types of viruses and malwares that, if given access to your computer, will take screenshots, steal passwords and corrupt your files. These kinds of attacks can be absolutely devastating, wiping out digital photo albums of precious memories, destroying information you need for your work and compromising the security of your entire online life.

It's Easy to Assume You're Not At Risk

The internet feels safe. We use it all the time, and that familiarity can make us feel like there's nothing to worry about. In the same way that you might drive to the shop to pick up some milk without much concern, it's second nature to head online to shop for a new phone case. However, you might be giving more away than you think with your harmless internet browsing.

You probably wouldn't go to the shop with money hanging out of your pocket, or leave your credit card out on a counter while you go for a walk around the shop. There are certain measures you take, almost without thinking about it, in your day-to-day life to keep yourself safe from opportunistic criminals.

You keep your money tucked away in a wallet or bag. You keep your passport, and other identifying documents, somewhere safe. You don't show strangers the security number on your credit card.

None of this is difficult, they're just common-sense precautions for going about your business without putting yourself at unnecessary risk.

Why Should You Understand Cybersecurity

There are a lot of similarly common-sense precautions you can take online, and they're not much more difficult than anything you'd do in the real world. The only real difference is that a lot of the risks you're exposed to (or exposing yourself to) online aren't as immediately obvious as leaving your car unlocked or leaving your wallet lying around.

Part of keeping safe online is learning how to recognize the dangers that exist, so you can put simple measures in place to protect yourself from them.

The following infographic illustrates some of the ways that you might be vulnerable as an internet user, without even being aware of it.

You Can't Afford to Get Hacked

CYBERSECURITY THREATS

5 KEY RISKS TO WATCH OUT FOR

PHISHING MESSAGES
BE WARY OF REQUESTS FOR PERSONAL INFO

More than 3 billion phishing messages are sent each and every day, making up half of all fraud attacks. Don't click on an email or message link if you aren't completely sure it's legitimate, and don't reply to unsolicited emails with personal information such as bank account details.

UNSECURED CONNECTIONS
INFORMATION CAN BE INTERCEPTED

When using a public or unsecured connection, bear in mind that anybody could be eavesdropping to gather information from what you're doing, potentially getting hold of your login details. Always avoid accessing personal information via an unsecured connection.

SUSPICIOUS DOWNLOADS
APPS AND ATTACHMENTS CAN HIDE MALWARE

An app or attachment might look legitimate, but it's important to double check before downloading anything. 48% of malicious email attachments are Microsoft Office files, because people are more likely to trust them. Never assume a download is safe.

WEBSITE TRACKERS
YOUR INFORMATION MIGHT BE FOR SALE

Websites can use cookies to track your use of their site, then sell that information on to others. Cookies can also stay in your browser long after you've left the site they came from. Be aware of what tracking permissions you give to sites, and clear your browser regularly.

SOCIAL MEDIA
BE AWARE OF HOW MUCH YOU SHARE

Your social media is full of useful information for a criminal, whether the end goal is identity fraud or selling on your personal information to a third party. Over half of social media logins are thought to be fraudulent. Protect your accounts with strong, unique passwords.

Sources:
VAILMAIL'S EMAIL FRAUD LANDSCAPE REPORT, Q2 2018
SYMANTEC'S 2019 INTERNET SECURITY THREAT REPORT
ARKOSE LABS' Q3 FRAUD AND ABUSE REPORT, 2019

Why Should You Understand Cybersecurity

There's a tendency for consumers to put too much faith in an antivirus program which, while important, can't do anything to protect you from scams, social engineering or many of the risks to your privacy that take place on a daily basis.

The information that you leave about yourself online is like a trail of breadcrumbs. Any one piece of information alone might not seem to put you in danger, but when put together they can be followed, leading to more and more of your personal data.

Imagine knowing that your name, address, credit card details, social security number, work history and medical records were completely available to anybody who decided to go looking.

It's a scary thought, but even scarier is how close to the truth it is. The internet contains a vast amount of information, much of it personal, and a lot of it is not protected as well as you would like it to be.

That's why it's up to users to learn the basics of cybersecurity, and protect their own personal information.

Everybody is potentially at risk online, but perhaps most at risk are children and young people, who might struggle to understand the possible consequences of sharing information online. Between convoluted privacy settings and constant encouragement to put as much of your life on the internet as you can, young people can become easy targets for scammers or, more worryingly, predators.

Our aim is not scare-mongering, but the fact remains there is a lot of risk associated with living so much of our lives online. Luckily, there are a number of simple and straightforward ways to keep yourself safe, protecting your private information, keeping your family safe, and avoiding scams.

Cybersecurity Is Complicated Though, Isn't It?

There's a misconception that protecting yourself online requires the equivalent of a computer science degree, but it really doesn't have to be that complicated. In this book, you are going to learn:

- How to protect yourself while using the internet in public spaces
- Simple steps to securing your personal information at home
- The safest ways to use social media, so you're not giving away more than you mean to
- Some of the most common cybersecurity threats and social engineering
- How to keep kids safe online

Everything within these pages is geared towards somebody with no prior knowledge of cybersecurity. You don't have to be an expert to protect yourself, you just need a basic understanding of the risks that are out there and the tools at your disposal.

It's all too common for people to overlook their online security until they're the victim of hacking, or they are infected with malware, at which point it's too late: the damage is done. Whoever you are—parent, office worker, freelance worker, entrepreneur, manager, life coach—you can't afford to get hacked. You're busy, you have things

Why Should You Understand Cybersecurity

to do, and you don't want a malicious cyber-attack to interfere with your life.

Luckily, all it takes is a few simple steps to make sure you're taking a proactive approach to your internet safety, and the safety of your family, and this guide will take you through every one of them.

Let's get started!

You Can't Afford to Get Hacked

Your Cybersecurity in Public

There is a moment of intense relief when you're sat somewhere in public—in a coffee shop, for example—and you see the sign: "Free Wi-Fi Available".

Whether you're waiting for a friend, taking a little break for yourself or killing time before the next meeting, it's nice to be able to check your emails or watch something on YouTube without having to worry about data usage.

Most of us have had the experience of connecting our laptop, tablet or mobile phone to a hotspot for a bit of free internet, but you might be unaware of the threats lurking in the background on public Wi-Fi while you stream some music and sip a coffee.

Imagine you're in an airport and decide to quickly check your emails before your flight, using public Wi-Fi. This seems like a harmless activity, but if a hacker takes the opportunity to steal your login details, you might land at your destination to find that a virus has been sent to everybody in your address book from your email account. This kind of scenario is unfortunately all too possible if using a public Wi-Fi connection.

In this chapter, we are going to cover:

- What risks you can encounter on public Wi-Fi
- How to keep yourself and your information as safe as possible if using public Wi-Fi
- How to recover if you are concerned you might have been hacked

Before we go into the type of threat you might be accidentally exposing yourself to on public Wi-Fi though, there are a few terms we should define.

What Is A Public Network?

A public network is a type of network that anybody can access in order to connect to other networks or the internet. It has few restrictions, or sometimes none at all, limiting who can connect to it. You often find public networks in places like airports, coffee shops and libraries.

Many hospitals have free public Wi-Fi now, which you might have noticed if you've had to spend a long time in a waiting room recently! Having public networks available in all of these places may feel like a convenience, but it's important to understand the possible risks associated with using these connections.

What Is A Public Station?

When we refer to a public station, what we mean is a computer in a public space that is available to rent or use by anybody. This includes computers in libraries, which can be used by any visitors, or in internet cafes.

If you've ever rented some time at a computer in an airport to get some work done before a flight, for example, you've used a public station! They can be convenient, but the fact that anybody can access them at any time makes them essentially unsecure.

What Is Public Wi-Fi?

This is Wi-Fi which you can find and connect to in public spaces, like malls, restaurants, coffee shops and hotels. With public Wi-Fi, you can access the internet for free. Some of these Wi-Fi networks ask for a password first, or require you to sign up with an email address, before you can use them. With others, you just have to be within range to connect, with no password required.

It might seem totally harmless to use public Wi-Fi to log into your social media account and post an update, read some emails or check your bank account, but performing any activity requiring you to log in to personal accounts can be risky through public Wi-Fi.

What Are The Risks?

Although providing Wi-Fi to customers is probably intended as a benefit, most public Wi-Fi networks have little to no security, and that results in a huge number of possible risks to users. Here are just a few of the dangers associated with using public Wi-Fi:

Man in the Middle, Snooping and Sniffing

> *"I used a public Wi-Fi connection the other day to send some money to a friend, but they told me later that they never got it. I checked my bank account and the money definitely went out, but my friend had a look later and told me I hadn't sent it to her bank account! I copied the information from the message exactly, but she said the message had been changed to somebody else's details before I got it. I had no idea a hacker could do that."*

A 'Man in the Middle' attack is an incredibly common way for criminals to take advantage of these open networks. Essentially, it's like eavesdropping. It involves a hacker putting themselves between your computer and the network you're connecting to, so that any information you send or receive from the internet goes via the hacker's device.

Let's say you're logging in to your online banking. You're not planning on sending any money, you just want to check your balance, so you're not worried about using public Wi-Fi.

Unfortunately, a hacker connected to the same Wi-Fi and carrying out a Man in the Middle attack can use this to see exactly what you're doing, including seeing any login information you filled out to get to your balance on the bank's website.

Not only can they see what's going on, a Man in the Middle attack can actively interfere with communication. For an example, see the illustration below. A hacker can use a Man in the Middle attack to intercept messages and provide incorrect information, in order to mislead people and steal money.

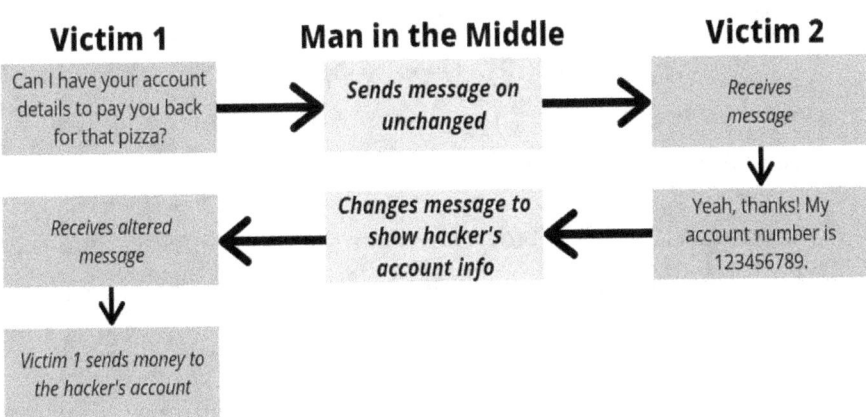

Snooping and sniffing are both similar. Hackers can use special devices or pieces of software to make it easier to eavesdrop on Wi-Fi signals, allowing them to access everything you do while connected to that network. Not only can they see the information you had to input to get access to your online banking, they can also see your credit card information and balance.

Not only do you probably not want strangers looking at your bank accounts, once they have your login information it becomes easy for them to get into your account at a later date.

Unencrypted networks

> *"I was doing some online shopping, when my laptop popped up with a notification saying that my connection wasn't private. I just ignored it and used my usual username and password to login. Now I'm locked out of all of my accounts, because apparently somebody has gone in and changed all my login details. I can't use any of my social media, and I can't get into my email account."*

'Encryption' is a kind of code. If a network is encrypted, it means that messages sent from your computer to the network are coded, so they cannot be read by eavesdroppers. Some websites are encrypted, so that any information sent between your computer and that website is kept private.

If a network is unencrypted, that means any information via that network is completely visible to anybody who might want to look at it.

Also, hackers can use an unencrypted Wi-Fi connection to send out malware. Malware is any software designed to cause damage to computers of mobile devices.

If file-sharing is allowed on your computer, a hacker can use the unsecured Wi-Fi connection to put infected software on your computer.

You can tell whether a website is using encryption by a padlock in the address bar, with the address starting with "HTTPS"—pay attention to that "s" at the end of HTTPS—and many browsers also use the color green to indicate that the website is protected. There are some examples of what it looks like in the image below.

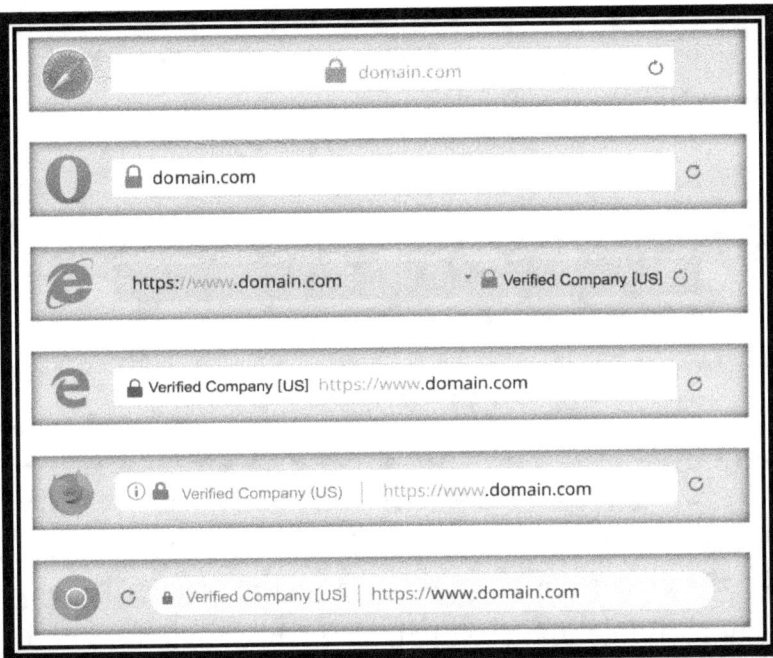

This means the website is safe to use, with minimal risk of hackers being able to see what you're doing on the site. Or at least, it should do.

While it is safe, in theory, to access encrypted websites without risk of prying eyes, there is software that makes it possible for hackers to hijack unsecured connections and make them *look* like secured ones.

If a website is not secure, you should see a warning message about it, such as the one in the image below. Even if you would normally trust the website, you should avoid using one with an unsecured connection if you are on public Wi-Fi.

You Can't Afford to Get Hacked

Even supposedly harmless information can be used by cyber-criminals, putting you at risk.

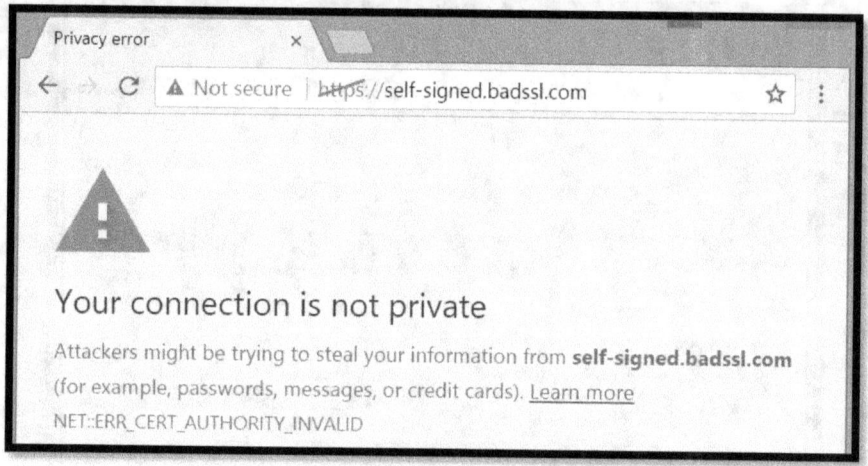

On an unencrypted network, using a virtual private network (or VPN) connection can be a good solution to create a layer of real protection. While using a VPN, all anybody will be able to tell about your internet activity is that you're connected to the VPN—your browsing will be secure.

It doesn't provide perfect protection from cyber-criminals; however, most hackers are on the lookout for an easy target. Even if a hacker were to stage a Man in the Middle attack, if you are using a VPN your data will be strongly encrypted.

You can buy a VPN account online from many companies, just make sure that VPN provider is reputable. Most antivirus brands will sell VPN accounts as well, and they are reliable and secure. Don't buy a VPN account from unknown or non-reputable providers, as they can play the role of Man in the Middle—this time securely over the VPN!

Malicious hotspots, or fake Wi-Fi

"I was relieved when I saw my hotel had Wi-Fi! I spent all evening watching YouTube videos on my laptop. There were some annoying pop-ups, but I just clicked 'okay' to make them go away. But when I turned on my laptop this morning, all my files were corrupted. I've lost so many photos, and a big work project I had almost finished. It's a disaster."

Some people will set up fake Wi-Fi networks with names that sound reputable to trick people into connecting.

For example, imagine you're staying at the Goodnyght Inn and you know they have free Wi-Fi. When you use your mobile phone to scan for available networks, you see a name that looks familiar and connect to "GoodnyteInn", assuming this is the correct one. It's an easy mistake to make but, if that has been set up by cyber-criminals, they can now observe everything you do using the internet, and potentially carry out attacks like the ones we have already discussed.

Even if the Wi-Fi is the 'official' public Wi-Fi for a building or public space, there is a chance it could have been compromised by cyber-criminals. Some hackers are able to hack the Wi-Fi connection point, so that when you connect to the network a pop-up window will appear which, if you click it, will install malware on your computer.

Unfortunately, there's really no way to know that your information is safe over public Wi-Fi.

> **Did you know?**
>
> According to a 2016 survey carried out by Symantec, 60% of American consumers believe that their information is safe while using public Wi-Fi.
>
> Of those people, only 50% believe they have a personal responsibility to protect their data.

How to Stay Safe on Public Wi-Fi

Ideally, you should completely avoid using public Wi-Fi to carry out any personal tasks or anything requiring a login.

Wherever possible, do not check your bank account, access emails or log into social media websites while on public Wi-Fi. In most cases, whatever you're planning to do or check can wait until you're at home, or somewhere else with a private, secured network.

If it's unavoidable to connect to public Wi-Fi while you're out and about, there are some actions you can take to protect your information:

- **Do** pay attention to any warnings that come up on your device to inform you that you might be connecting to unsecured networks or websites.
- **Don't** allow your laptop or mobile device to automatically connect to Wi-Fi or other networks. You can usually make sure this is disabled quite easily by going into your phone or

Your Cybersecurity in Public

laptop settings and turning off any option that relates to automatic connection.

- **Do** make sure that, if you're not using Wi-Fi or Bluetooth, your devices are not scanning for those networks. Again, you can stop your devices from looking for these connections using the connectivity settings.
- **Don't** log onto a network without password protection. As convenient as it might seem to log onto public Wi-Fi without having to enter a password, this means it is that much easier for hackers to get access to peoples' internet activity while connected to that network.
- **Do** make sure you're only visiting sites using HTTPS while connected to public Wi-Fi. This means sites with the little padlock in the address bar. This adds an important extra layer of privacy when you're using the internet.
- **Don't** have a false sense of security though. Even if a site is encrypted (meaning it has the padlock), remember you can't be completely sure that it's secure. Hackers can trick your device into recognizing an unsecured website as a secure one.
- **Do** make sure to log out of accounts when you're done using them, to make it as difficult as possible for hackers to obtain access to your accounts.
- **Don't** put yourself at unnecessary risk. As much as possible, avoid accessing any websites that store sensitive information about you, such as financial or healthcare information.
- **Do** consider using a VPN from a VPN service provider, which will make sure your public Wi-Fi connections are

made private. Just make sure that you select a VPN from a reliable provider, such as from your preferred antivirus company. Not all VPN providers are legitimate.

- **Don't** use the same password on more than one site. If a hacker is able to get your login information for one of your sites, having separate passwords for every login will limit the places they can access your information.
- **Do** ensure file sharing is disabled on your computer. This might be convenient at home, allowing you to keep files in a folder shared with other members of your household, but if you're connecting to public Wi-Fi you don't want strangers to be able to access your files—or share potentially infected files with you. You can disable file sharing through the control panel on Windows devices, or system preferences if using a Mac.
- **Don't** send emails containing sensitive information, either in the body of the email or as an attachment.
- **Do** make sure you have up-to-date antivirus software installed on your computer.

What If You Suspect You've Been Hacked?

If you're concerned that you might have been hacked, there are some important steps you should take to minimize the possible damage:

- Use a computer that you're confident has not been compromised to login to your accounts and reset your passwords.

Your Cybersecurity in Public

- Make sure you are logged out of any devices that you have allowed to remember you. If you're not sure how to do this, you can do an internet search for "log out of all devices [Facebook/Instagram/Gmail/etc.]" to find a step-by-step pictorial guide.
- If you have any problems with your online banking system, call your bank's support team via telephone. Make sure you get their phone number from the bank's official website, do not call a number received via a text or email message, and **do not** give your online banking password to the operator.

Protect Yourself As Well As You Can

Being armed with proper information about the security of public Wi-Fi networks will help you to stay safe online. There may well be times when you need to do work requiring an internet connection, and unsecured public Wi-Fi is the only option.

Now, you have an understanding of the risks, and steps you can take to protect yourself, to prevent your important work data or personal information falling into the hands of cyber-criminals.

You Can't Afford to Get Hacked

Securing Your Personal Information at Home

There's nowhere we feel more secure than at home, and it's easy to assume that being connected to our own, private router means that we're safe online. While it's true that a lot of risks are significantly reduced when you're using the internet at home, there are still a lot of things to keep an eye out for, and a lot of things you should be doing to make sure that you and your family are staying safe online

Shopping and Banking Online

Both of these activities involve your sensitive financial information being sent over the internet, so it's vital you make sure you're as safe as possible when buying online or accessing your online banking. If a hacker were to get access to your financial information, it could be devastating, so it's important to take precautions. Some of the basic measures include:

- Only ever doing your online shopping or banking when connected to a secure, private network.
- Making sure you do any online shopping through well-known and trusted websites.
- Regularly checking your bank statements and transactions to be sure you recognize everything that's come into or left your account.

Hopefully you're doing most of this already, but this is really the bare minimum in terms of cybersecurity for online shopping and banking. Either way, we're going to take you through some more specific actions you can take to really make sure you're protecting your financial information online.

Don't allow websites or browsers to save your card details

No matter how convenient it sounds, never save your card details online. Whether to your browser, your preferred online retailers or your accounts with ecommerce stores. Whenever you make a purchase, whether it's on Amazon, eBay, ASOS or Etsy, you should input your card information manually each and every time. The time you save by having the browser or website remember your payment details simply isn't worth the increased risk of fraud.

If one of these accounts is breached—which could happen for a whole range of reasons, from an error or poor luck on your part, to a cyber-attack on the company holding your account information—

a cyber-criminal could get access to your card information and use it freely.

Check for key security elements before completing transactions

Before you go through with any online payment or login to your online banking, there are a few specifics you should make sure of.

1. Make sure the website has the padlock symbol and that the web address starts with https. This means the website is encrypted, so the data transferred is protected from eavesdroppers.
2. Double check the spelling of the URL to make sure you are on the official website. If you haven't used the website before, you can do a Google search to verify the correct web address and be sure you're in the right place.
3. Watch out for any new or unusual steps to your login process. Again, if you're using a site for the first time, there are some specifics to watch out for: your bank will not ask you for your address, card number or PIN as part of the login process. If at any point during your login or transaction you feel like something isn't right, leave the website, use an official contact number to speak to customer service for the company and find out how you can finish your transaction safely.
4. Carefully inspect the visual elements of the page, particularly the site's logo. When criminals are setting up fake sites to try to capture information, they sometimes take these images

You Can't Afford to Get Hacked

from the web to try to make their version look legitimate. You should be looking for any fuzziness, or outdated versions of the company's logo or branding imagery; these indicate that the site you're on might not be the real one. If something does seem off to you, a Google search for the official website can help you confirm your suspicions.

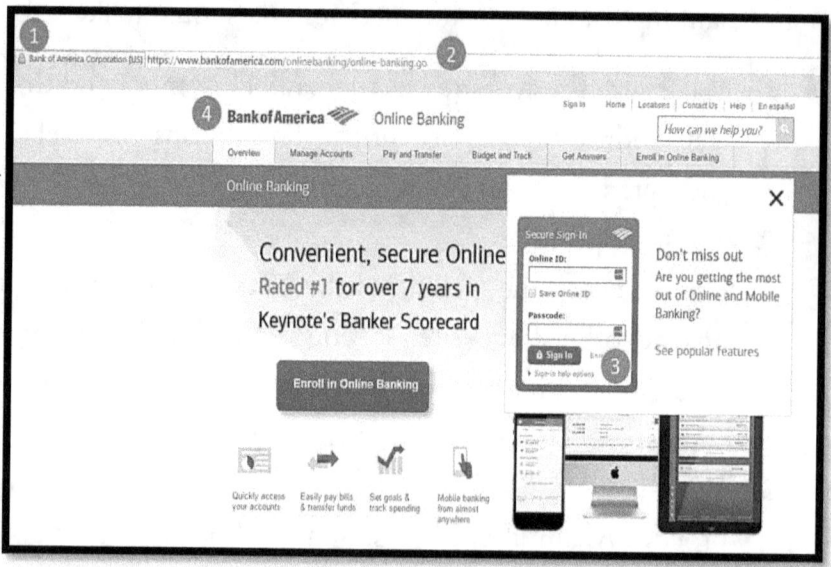

If you do find yourself on a fake site while trying to access your online banking, make sure to contact the bank—using contact information from a separate source, of course—to inform them of it.

Make sure you're also on the lookout for 'spoofed' website URLs, these are versions of a website with a slightly different name, such as the below example of 'amazonn.com'. These might look similar to the real thing, but that subtle difference in spelling will take you to a completely different site.

Type out URLs manually, and be sure to check them for any errors before you go ahead with your transactions.

Protecting Your Passwords

Your password is the first line of defense when somebody tries to get access to one of your accounts, but a staggering number of people aren't taking the most basic precautions with their online passwords. The first, most basic, piece of advice you'll hear about passwords is this:

Never reuse passwords.

None of your accounts, from your work email to your YouTube account to your login for MyFitnessPal, should use the same password. In the first half of 2019 alone, 4.1 *billion* records were exposed as a result of data breaches[2].

If one of those records was yours, a hacker could have your password. If that's just the password to one social media site, it's a problem. If that's your password to everything though? It's a disaster.

> **Did you know?**
> 65% of people use the same password for multiple accounts, sometimes even all of their accounts, according to a 2019 online security survey by Google.

Compromised passwords are the root cause of around 80% of hacking-related breaches[3], and using the same password for multiple accounts makes life considerably easier for hackers who can take the information from one attack and use it to steal data, information or even your money by using that information to login to any number of additional accounts.

Once you've resolved to never use the same password twice (really, absolutely never), you also need to make sure you're using suitably

---

[2] That's an increase of 52% compared to the number of records exposed through breaches in the same period in 2018, as reported in Risk Based Security's 2019 Mid-Year Data Breach Report. This problem is only getting worse.
[3] 81%, according to Verizon's 2018 Data Breach Incident Report

strong passwords. There are a lot of common mistakes that people make when choosing a password, so here are some things that make **terrible** passwords, which you should avoid at all costs:

- The word 'password', or any variation of it. That includes 'password123' or 'passw0rd'.
- The word 'admin', or anything like it.
- Any part or variation of your own name.
- Your own date of birth, or location of birth.
- Any part or variation of your partner's name, or their date of birth.
- Any part of variation of the name of *any* family member, or birthdays. Including your pets.
- A non-random sequence of numbers, such as 123456, 987654321, 00000, etcetera.

All of these are predictable and, therefore, unsafe. Using any one of them is like leaving your car unlocked, with the key in the ignition.

A strong password is of a suitable length, involving a combination of letters, both uppercase and lowercase, numbers and special characters (things like £, & and *). A good example might be: **Da*F6q$%t^10(**. Although obviously don't use that one!

The problem with passwords like this is that the same things that make them so strong—they're long, complicated and random—also make them incredibly difficult to remember. And this is a good time to introduce another golden rule of passwords:

Don't write your passwords down.

Now, if you're thinking you may as well give up now, because you'll never be able to remember strong passwords without having them written down somewhere, we have a solution.

You can use triggers which you'll find easy to remember, to create strong passwords which still contain enough complexity to be strong and secure. For example, let's say the first song you danced to at your wedding was 'All of Me', by John Legend. Hopefully you won't forget that in a hurry! The first line of the song goes like this: **'What would I do without your smart mouth?'**

Now, you can use the first letter of each of those words to create a string of characters, like this: **Wwidwysm?** Then you could decide to replace some of the letters with numbers or special characters. Maybe all of the lowercase 'w's become ^ instead, and you swap out the 'i' for a 1. That gives you: **W^1d^ysm?** A much more secure password!

Using Antivirus

Installing good antivirus software is a core component of cybersecurity, but don't be fooled: it can't protect you against everything. Cyber-criminals are always working on more sophisticated techniques, trying to out-smart your antivirus.

Antivirus can also only work as well as you let it; it can't protect you if its database isn't kept up to date and, if you open an infected attachment or click on a compromised link, you'll be inviting malware onto your device despite the best efforts of your antivirus.

Hackers frequently use phishing messages to try to trick you into giving away personal information (you'll learn more about phishing messages later in this book) and antivirus can't help you avoid those.

Of course, none of that is to say you shouldn't bother with antivirus. Antivirus is important, make no mistake! And you need to make sure you get a good one installed. There are some reasonably effective free antivirus options available, but the paid options will usually provide you far more complete protection.

Whether you're going for a paid or free antivirus software, have a look at reviews online and choose from one of the known, reliable brands. Some trusted examples include Bitdefender, Norton, Kaspersky, Avast and Avira.

Watch out for fake antivirus

Hackers love to exploit people's anxieties about viruses to infect their computers. If you ever come across a pop-up or email claiming, "Your device has been infected! Click this link to download NEWANTIVIRUS so your device will be protected!" you should delete and ignore it.

No genuine antivirus company will send you that kind of message, and the chances are high that clicking that link will download malware or a virus, to steal or corrupt the information on your device.

Maintaining Good Email Security

Take a moment to think about how much you rely on email. Many of us use it for sending and receiving important documents, confirming personal information, keeping in touch with people we care about, and so much more. If somebody were to hack into your email, they would have access to all of that, and be able to use it or delete it at will.

To keep your email accounts as safe as possible, you need to look into each of the following:

Recovery information

This is vital for getting your account back if it's hacked, or if you've forgotten your password. Your email provider will have its own ways to set up recovery, but some typical examples are:

- Through another email account
- By sending a limited-time passcode to your mobile phone
- With security questions you can set up with specific answers

Your email activity log

Many email account providers allow you to check a recent activity log for your account, so that you can see what devices and browsers have accessed the account, when the account was accessed and which IP address the access came from.

If you spot an access that you don't recognize as one of your own, it's a simple matter of terminating that access, so the session is ended.

Securing Your Personal Information at Home

Of course, in that case you'll want to take additional steps to ensure your email account can't be accessed again, but we'll cover those in a moment.

This isn't limited to email either, many other online accounts for social media or data storage have the same feature.

You should make a habit of checking your activity logs for email accounts on a regular basis, such as every couple of weeks, to ensure there's nothing shady going on.

Two-factor authentication

You should activate two-factor authentication on every account that will allow you to do so, as it provides an important second layer of protection after your password.

For email accounts, this is often done with a mobile phone number or app. Once set up, whenever you want to log in to your email account from a device or browser that you haven't used before you will be asked for an additional code. This will come to your mobile phone, and will only be valid for a limited time.

This means that, even if somebody were to get your email password, they couldn't get into your account without also having access to your phone at the precise moment they wanted to log in.

What should you do if you believe your account was involved in a breach?

If you think somebody may have had access to your email account—for example, maybe you saw a suspicious login when you checked the activity log—the first thing you should do is change your password for the effective account as soon as possible. Make sure the new password is strong, unique, and completely unrelated to the one you used before.

Set up two-factor authentication, if you hadn't already, to ensure nobody can get into your account without having an additional, secondary code sent to your phone.

Also, if that password was in use anywhere else (which we've established it **should never be**), connect to those other accounts and change those passwords as well. To unique ones, this time!

There are a couple of databases you can search to check whether your email address has been involved in a data breach:

- www.haveibeenpwned.com
- www.breachalarm.com

Data breaches happen on pretty much a daily basis, and there's a good chance you'll be a victim of one at some point. Don't panic, just take the steps outlined here, and you can limit the damage—in most cases to little more than inconvenience.

Using USBs

You might occasionally find that you come across a USB device (sometimes called a thumb drive, or USB stick) that seems to have been lost by somebody.

Being a helpful and honest person, you might want to find out who it belongs to so that you can make sure it's returned. And the immediately obvious way to do that is to plug the USB device into your computer to look for some indication of who the owner is.

Unfortunately, that's a terrible idea.

The USB device could well have been left behind deliberately by a cyber-criminal. In that case, the moment you plug the device in you can immediately find yourself in trouble.

> **Did you know?**
>
> Nearly 50% of people who come across a discarded or lost USB device will plug it into their own computer and look at the files, according to research done by the University of Illinois and University of Michigan.

There are a few common ways hackers can use USB sticks to cause problems, for example:

- Clicking on any of the files stored on the drive could activate malicious code, which might introduce a virus to corrupt your files, download malware from the internet or send the hacker private information stored on your computer.
- A file on the device could direct you to a phishing site, designed to trick you into putting in login information which the cyber-criminal can then use to access your accounts.

- The device could have been made to act like a keyboard, but look like a USB device. This means you computer might interpret it as a keyboard, allowing the hacker to use it to issue commands to your computer from wherever they are, or capture your keystrokes to see any passwords you type.

Some Additional Things to Remember

Here are a few more quick cybersecurity tips to keep in mind while using the internet at home.

Cover or disconnect your webcam

If your laptop comes with a built-in webcam, you should make sure it's covered when not in use. If you have a webcam plugged in to your computer or laptop, you should disconnect it when you don't actively need it.

This might sound paranoid, but technology and computer experts will almost universally give you the same advice; you just never know who might be watching.

Make sure your internet browsers are kept up to date

Do a regular check for any available updates to your browser, as well as any add-ons or plugins you use with it.

Software developers release updates to fix bugs, and shore up any areas where the program might be weak to outside interference. Rejecting or ignoring updates can lead to security holes that hackers can (and will) take advantage of.

In 2017 a wide-scale ransomware attack called "NotPetya" spread across Europe. It was targeting the exact same vulnerability that a different attack (called "WannaCry") used to cause chaos just a month earlier. If people and companies had kept their software up to date, neither of those attacks could have caused the chaos that they did—Microsoft had released an update which closed up that gap in security *two months* before the first attack.

Updates can come at inconvenient times, and it's annoying to have to stop what you're doing while your computer runs updates, but it's better than the alternative.

Watch out for unsupported software

It's not unusual to come across news articles stating that a company has 'discontinued support' for a specific software, but what does this mean?

Ending support for a software means that the developer will no longer be keeping that software going through sales, marketing or—most importantly—support. There will be no further updates released to add features or improve performance or security.

Hopefully, having already read about the importance of keeping your browsers updated, you can see why this could be a problem!

As hackers and criminals develop new tools and techniques for attacking software, developers need to update their software to repel those attacks. If an app or program that you use is no longer being updated, any new vulnerabilities will be left wide open for cyber-criminals to exploit.

The only way around this is to never use unsupported software, and ensure your applications are kept up to date.

Phone Security

Even people who are relatively on top of cybersecurity for their laptops or home computers can have a tendency to overlook the security for their phone. But think for a moment about how much you use your phone, and how much sensitive information is stored on it.

Many of the tips we've already covered will apply just as easily to your mobile phone, but here are some more phone-specific pieces of advice:

- Keep your phone's screen lock feature on at all times.
- Use the connectivity settings on your phone to turn off Wi-Fi and Bluetooth when you're not using them.
- When installing a new app, carefully read the permissions it's asking for, and don't allow blanket permissions without reason. If an app is asking to use your gallery, camera or microphone, consider whether that is actually necessary for that app before saying yes.
- Don't jailbreak or root your phone. This can open you up to a whole host of vulnerabilities which hackers can easily exploit. It's also, in many cases, against the terms and conditions of use of your device, so if you run into any problems down the line you won't be protected by your warranty.

- Don't install apps from unknown sources. Use official apps from legitimate developers, downloaded from trusted app stores.
- Make a habit of regularly backing up your data on a cloud service, the most popular options for this are probably either Apple iCloud or Google Cloud. This will allow you to restore your data down the line if your phone is compromised.

Watch out for mobile apps

We already mentioned the importance of restricting your downloading of apps to official stores and developers. You can disable the option to allow installation of third-party apps, this will mean you can't download apps from friends online, internet ads, blogs or torrents—all of which are more likely to come with malware which can damage or compromise the security of your phone.

That doesn't mean that apps and games from official stores come completely without risk. Even popular apps from trustworthy developers can turn out to have vulnerabilities that cyber-criminals are able to take advantage of.

You Can't Afford to Get Hacked

> **Did you know?**
> 76% of mobile applications have insecure data storage, according to a 2018 report by Positive Technologies. This kind of vulnerability can put passwords, financial information and personal data at risk.

Make sure you're only downloading what you really need, and only keeping what you really need. If an app is gathering dust on your home screen, uninstall it from your phone. And always be mindful when using apps that the security of any photos or messages you send can't be guaranteed.

Don't get rid of your phone without doing a factory reset

If you're thinking of selling, donating or just binning your old phone, make sure you do a full Factory Data Reset first.

This will wipe all of the information that was stored on it, including any access you granted the device to personal accounts; data and settings from the phone system and apps; any photos, videos, files or data stored in the phone's memory. Everything.

Perform a backup first, so you don't risk losing anything, and then carry out the Factory Reset so that the next owner can't get any information about you from the device.

You can typically find the option for a Factory Reset in the settings of your phone.

Nothing Is Free on The Internet

You know the classic saying, 'There's no such thing as a free lunch'? Well, this is as true online as it is everywhere else. If an app or piece of software is free to use, you need to think about how the developer is making their money. There's a good chance it's by selling your personal data. And even if it's supported by ads, there might be significant risks you're exposing yourself to by accessing these services.

Free streaming

Streaming is a convenient way to catch up on TV shows or listen to music, and there are a huge number of websites allowing you to do all this for free. Great! Right? Well, maybe not. Pirated streaming services see an enormous amount of traffic, more than 120 billion visits in 2017[4], but these websites are like a playground for cyber-criminals.

They are full of misleading pop-ups or adverts which, if clicked on, can prompt your computer to download a virus. Logging onto a streaming site can expose you to phishing as well, as you might find yourself accidentally redirected to a site that looks identical to the

---

[4] 73.9 billion visits to sites to pirate music and 53.2 billion visits to sites to illegally stream music in 2017, according to research by Muso.

original but which will actually try to steal your personal information.

File converters

There are a wide range of 'free' online file converters available online, for changing your PDF into a Word document or your mp4 into an mp3. These require you to upload your file onto their server, then download the converted file.

This comes with a couple of inherent risks. For one thing, once you've uploaded your file, you can't know what will happen to it. Perhaps the service claims that all uploaded files are deleted as soon as the conversion is done, but can you verify that? Be wary of this, and make sure you don't use an online converter for any private or sensitive files.

The other concern is safety. When you download your converted file, it might come with along with a virus or malware.

Some file converter websites ask for your email address, which might seem harmless enough, but they may well be selling that on to marketers looking for email lists—opening you up to a whole new world of spam emails.

Free software packages to download

Some of the risks associated with free software downloads are probably obvious to you by now. Fake download buttons on the download pages can be downloads of malware or spyware which can compromise your computer; the installer that comes with the program file might force you to install additional applications, including malware; malicious software updates can come out for free software packages, making your data insecure.

You can mitigate some of these risks by only downloading free software from trusted developers, by carefully reading through any permissions you're allowing and exactly what you're choosing to install, and by being very careful of where you're clicking on download pages for software.

Smart Home

When we talk about a smart home, we mean a home which uses devices connected to the internet, such as light switches, thermostats and fridges. These can be set up so that lights go on and off at pre-set times, doors can be locked or opened with a click of a button, your home heating can be adjusted with your phone as you leave work for the day, or you can get an alert to let you know you're low on milk. As wildly convenient as all of this is, it comes with some pretty significant risks.

Smart home devices can be riddled with security holes, making them vulnerable to hacking that can put your data at risk. And not just your data—if a hacker gains access to an internet-connected device which controls the lock to your front door, that puts your physical property at risk as well. And if that threat isn't bad enough, connected baby monitors can also be hacked and accessed remotely, allowing the hacker to speak to your child.

You Can't Afford to Get Hacked

Unfortunately, a comprehensive guide to the security of these devices is beyond the scope of this book. There are at least as many security threats as there are smart devices, and we just aren't able to cover all aspects of them within this guide. We can, however, go through some of the most important actions you can take to ensure devices in your home that connect to the internet are as secure as possible.

The Apple homepod

We're starting with a very specific one, because this is a good example of the kind of threat that can come with these kinds of devices. Apple's homepod uses Siri to respond to verbal requests but, unlike the version of Siri you'll find on your iPhone or iPad, the Siri on Apple's homepod does not differentiate between your voice and another person's (at the time of writing this book). To ensure that other people can't ask for personal information, such as reading new messages or looking through appointments in your calendar, make sure that your homepod's settings for personal requests is disabled through your iPhone.

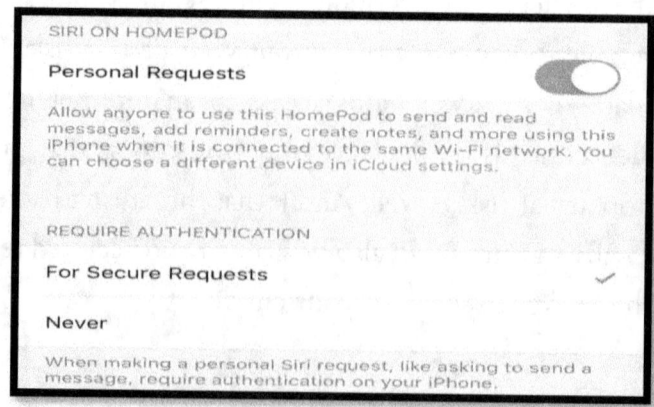

Name your router

Routers come with names provided by the manufacturer, but you should make sure to rename them as soon as possible. The default name can identify the make or model of your router, so if there are any known security vulnerabilities for your router a hacker will know exactly what to target.

Make sure the name you give doesn't give away any identifying information, such as your name or address.

Make sure your Wi-Fi network is encrypted

You can check your router settings to look at what encryption method is currently in place to protect information being passed through it. To make sure the network, and anything connected to it, is as secure as possible, you want to use a strong encryption method. WPA2 is a good option.

Set up a specific guest network

Rather than allowing visiting friends, relatives, coworkers etc to have access to your Wi-Fi account, you can set up a guest network. This limits how many people have the access information for the network that your smart devices are connected to, making them more secure.

Don't keep the default login details

Default passwords for smart devices are frequently well-known by cyber-criminals. As soon as you get a new device, change the default username and password to something unique and secure. You might want to employ our earlier advice on choosing a strong password!

Some devices don't allow you to change the password they come with. We recommend you don't buy these—the risk of being hacked is significantly higher.

Make sure your passwords for Wi-Fi networks and devices are strong and unique

You probably don't need a reminder of this, but don't use common words for your passwords, or any easy-to-discover personal information about yourself or your family. All of your passwords should be unique—don't reuse passwords across different smart devices—and should be complex passwords made up of letters, symbols and numbers.

Check privacy settings on your devices

There will probably be settings you can tweak on your smart devices for privacy or security, and it's worth having a look through these when you first activate the product. Some of these settings, around information sharing, are allowed by default because they can be useful to the manufacturer. Turn off all sharing for maximum security.

Disable features that you don't need or won't use

Functionality such as remote access might be enabled by default, but carefully consider whether that's something you're actually going to use. If not, turn it off to increase the security of the device against hacking.

Always make sure your device software is up to date

You might get notifications from the manufacturer when a new update is available, or you may have to go to their websites to check. Make it a regular routine to go through all of your devices and check whether there are any new updates available, as these may well be fixes for security flaws.

Regularly check that your current devices are suitable

Sometimes you might need to upgrade to a newer model of a device to ensure continued security on your home network, either because support for the existing model has been discontinued or because newer versions are designed to offer superior security.

Put two-factor authentication in place

Make sure that you've set up two-factor authentication for every smart device app that offers it; this makes it significantly harder for a cyber-criminal to get access to your account.

Don't use public Wi-Fi

For all the same reasons we discussed earlier, you don't want to manage your smart devices while connected to public Wi-Fi. If it's an absolute necessity, you can take the steps we outlined there, such as using a VPN for enhanced security over public Wi-Fi networks.

Be mindful of outages

Make sure that any hardware outage or interruption of the power supply doesn't accidentally leave your device in an unsecured state.

Internet-connected devices can provide a huge amount of convenience, and they can be a lot of fun as well! Just make sure that you're using them safely, and taking every precaution to make sure these devices don't invite trouble into your home.

Don't Give Away More Than You Mean to on Social Media

Social media can be a wonderful thing. It keeps you connected with friends and family, wherever they are in the world. It helps you keep up with work colleagues, past and present, and even total strangers whose lives you might have a passing interest in.

The things that you share on social media can end up being circulated around the internet in a heartbeat, reaching all corners of the world, and this can be a great thing—if you're a business looking for clients, or interested in being internet-famous—but it can also be embarrassing or even devastating, depending on the circumstances.

There are security settings for many social media platforms that allow you to share your thoughts, pictures and so on with more privacy, however people who want to get access to this information can often find a way.

It's easy to think it isn't a big deal if your social media account is hacked. After all, it's not like they've got into your bank account, or taken your Social Security number! However, the information available through your Facebook account can be equally damaging if it falls into the wrong hands.

This is why it's important that you fully understand cybersecurity for social media.

What's the Danger?

Any hack of any account is cause for concern. If somebody has got into an account of yours, that is a breach of your personal information, and even if the hacker hasn't got into your bank accounts or anything that seems that obviously important, it's still a stranger who could be anywhere in the world with access to information you probably wouldn't have chosen to share with them. And the problem with strangers getting access to social media is that there's often a lot more information than you realize in there.

From the basic identification stuff—like your birthday, phone number and where you live—to the security questions you have set up—first pet's name, the street you grew up on, your mother's maiden name—social media accounts are a treasure trove of information to a hacker.

Don't forget, if they have access to your account that also means they can see all of the messages you've sent and received through it, so any personal information, photos or videos you've sent are now visible to them.

Additionally, if you've ever bought something through social media outlets your credit card information may well be stored.

Hopefully this is starting to clarify why you should keep your social media accounts as carefully guarded as you can!

What Goes Online, Stays Online

As with so many elements of cybersecurity, keeping safe on social media begins with being mindful of how you use it. Whenever you post to social media, consider the fact that almost anybody could end up seeing what you've uploaded there—not just your friends and family.

Your current employers might be able to see what you post, or any potential future employers, and a careless social media post can destroy a positive reputation. Maybe that sounds dramatic, but there have been cases of people losing their jobs for posting something on their private social media accounts—outside of work hours, and unrelated to their company.

In 2013 a PR Executive with only 170 followers tweeted an ignorant and insensitive joke before boarding a flight to South Africa. While on the flight, without her knowledge, the tweet went viral. It was seen by hundreds of thousands of people, and by the time she landed she had an avalanche of text messages and emails—including one from her manager letting her know she was fired.

When you post online:

- Make sure not to reveal too many personal details. Remember, most of those 'About Me' fields on your profile page are optional.

- Don't share anything personally embarrassing, or anything that would embarrass somebody else. Only post things that you'd be happy to say to peoples' faces, and that you don't mind being visible to everybody. It's also worth paying attention to what people post about you.
- Remember that sites like Twitter are, by default, open to anybody.
- Be mindful of the fact that anything you post online will be retrievable forever, and even deleting something isn't always enough to make it go away. If others have made a screenshot or saved something, it can keep popping back up long after you've tried to forget about it.

Oversharing and Identity Theft

Oversharing is everywhere on social media—people making too much information about themselves available to strangers or the general public. Of course, oversharing can happen either online or offline! The issue is that social media makes it so much easier to overshare—in many cases, actively encouraging it.

Most people love to share through social media. And who can blame them! The whole system is set up to make it as engaging as possible to share your life. But oversharing can have serious consequences for your online security, making you an attractive target for cyber-criminals.

Don't Give Away More Than You Mean to on Social Media

> **Did you know?**
> A survey by Nationwide Building Society in the UK found that more than 4 in 10 people had lost money as a result of a social media hack, or knew somebody else who had.

Using information from social media oversharing, cyber-criminals can attack and compromise your accounts, empty your bank accounts and send spam or malware from your email account.

Your Online Accounts Are All Connected

People don't generally give a lot of thought to how interconnected their online accounts are, but when you do examine it, you'll gain a new understanding of why cyber-criminals are keen to get access to something as seemingly harmless as an Instagram account.

The image below illustrates the ways your different social media and other online accounts link to each other, allowing a hacker who accesses one to find their way into all of the others without too much difficulty. It also highlights the kinds of information a cyber-criminal can find and make use of in each account.

You Can't Afford to Get Hacked

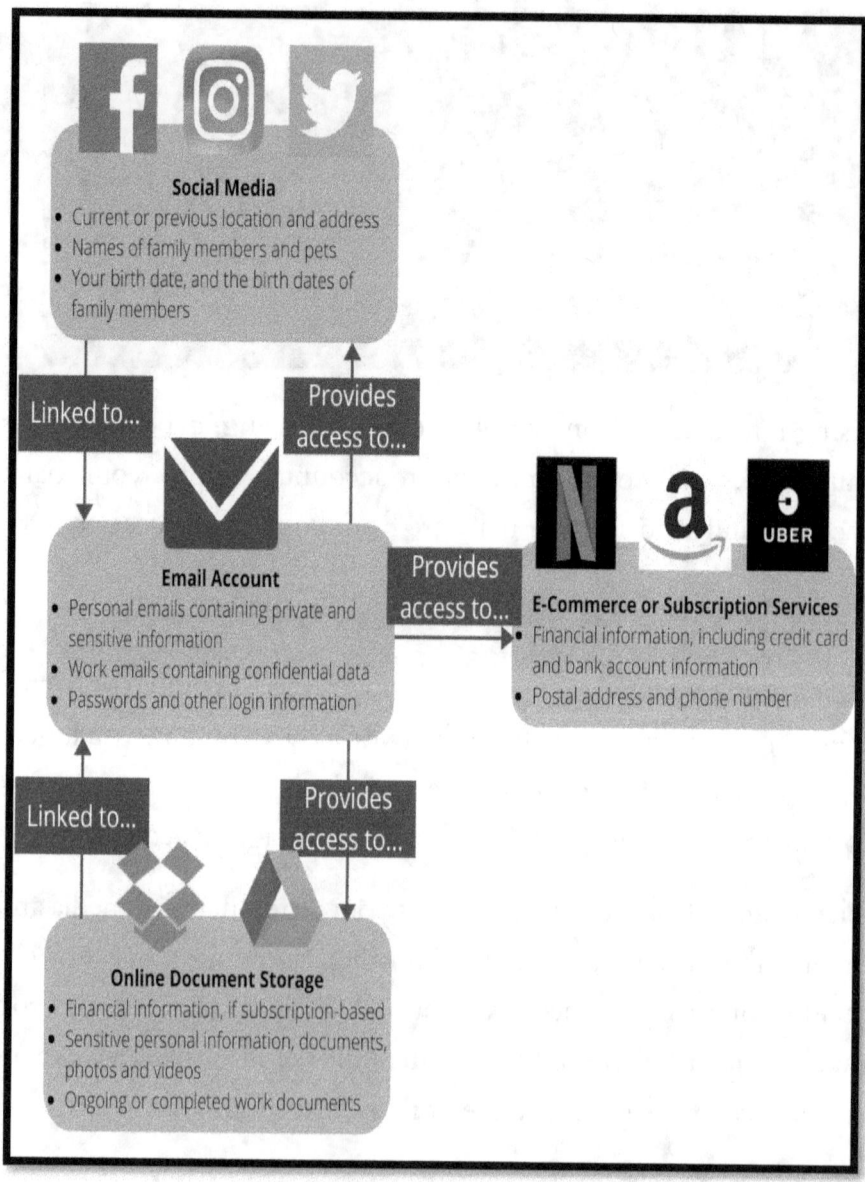

Getting into a social media account like Facebook or Instagram provides your email address, as well as a huge amount of personal data that can make it easier for a hacker to guess your passwords or security questions.

From there, it's significantly easier for them to get into your email account, which gives them access to crucial information about all of your other online accounts—as well as private information from your work and personal life.

If a cyber-criminal uses your email account to get access to your Amazon account, for example, they can get their hands on your shipping address and maybe even credit card details.

You might not think you have any valuable information in your social media accounts, but criminals are expert at finding ways to make money from information you don't think is important enough to protect.

How Can You Protect Yourself?

Update privacy and security settings

Take a tour through the privacy and security settings for every online account you have. It shouldn't be difficult to find these. Consider who you want your social media profiles to be visible to, and how much information you want to be available to them, and adjust your settings accordingly.

It's also worth going back periodically to check your settings, as they can be updated and changed as privacy policies are adjusted.

Two-factor authentication

We discussed the importance of this security measure in the previous chapter, but it bears repeating. Two-factor authentication adds a vital extra layer of protection to your accounts.

Once you enter your password on a new device, you'll receive a one-off code (usually to your phone) to ensure it's actually you attempting to access the account.

You should ensure that two-factor authentication is in place on every online account that will allow it—and it's becoming available on more and more platforms, as developers adopt this as security best-practice.

Site-specific social media privacy settings

Some cybersecurity principles apply pretty much universally, but it's also important to bear in mind that different sites have inherent differences, in terms of both the settings available to you and the way you might want to use those platforms.

On a site like Facebook, the central premise is based around connecting with friends, and so it makes a lot of sense to lock down your account and posts so that they are only visible to people you know and trust.

With other sites, the intention is built more around trading your privacy for greater reach and visibility. For example, sharing your views and thoughts far and wide through Twitter, or networking with people you don't necessarily have a personal connection with through LinkedIn.

Only you can decide what trade-offs you're willing to make while using social media sites. We recommend closely examining the various options available to you on each account that you use, so that you can make informed choices about your privacy settings. Choose your options based on your own priorities, and the way in which you use your social media, and just be conscious of what you choose to share on platforms where your privacy settings are less locked down.

Tips for Securing Your Social Media

The way we use social media varies wildly person to person, but there are some tips that everybody should be applying—whether they're hoping to land a new job through LinkedIn or trying to become the next great Instagram influencer.

Never share or re-use passwords

This is another tip that we've covered elsewhere, but it's so important that we're mentioning it again. Every account you have should have a totally unique password, and you should not give those passwords out to anybody else.

Passwords are your first line of defense—make sure they're as strong as possible!

You Can't Afford to Get Hacked

Make sure accounts are as secure as possible

This includes by taking the usual password precautions, but also by making sure two-factor authentication is set up wherever it's available. Set up security questions to allow you to recover your account using information only you have, and make sure your privacy settings are locked down as much as possible.

Turn on login notifications

This is another great precaution to take with your online accounts: turn on any function that will notify you if a new device accesses your accounts. This helps you keep control of your social media.

Be mindful of what you're sharing

Limit your posting of personal information wherever possible, and never share information that can be used as answers to security questions—such as the schools you've attended, birth date, names of family members and pets, where you've lived over the course of your life, and so on.

This can stray into the realm of real-world home security as well. If you're excited about an upcoming vacation, sharing exactly when you leave and how long you'll be gone, that's a great opportunity for potential thieves. Limiting the information you share about your life may not sound like fun, but it's a sensible precaution to take.

Don't click on suspicious ads or links

Ads, or messages containing links, can take you to pages that look like the same social media platform, but have in fact been set up by cyber-criminals to trick you into handing over login information.

Log out of accounts when not in use

Don't leave yourself logged in when you're done using any of your social media or other online accounts. Having a strong password and two-factor authentication isn't going to be any use to you if somebody can just open your laptop and pick up where you left off!

Fully close down old accounts

If you have set up accounts on social media platforms that you no longer use, like Bebo or Myspace, make sure they're fully shut down and deleted. There's no advantage to having your personal information hanging around on the internet in places you no longer visit.

Social Media Can Be Great

... As long as you use it carefully, and don't let it compromise your online security! Because it's so widely used, people have a tendency to let their guard down around these platforms. But hopefully you're now armed with an awareness of what the risks are and how you can best protect yourself.

You Can't Afford to Get Hacked

Scam Alert! Do Not Be the Victim of a Fraud!

In this chapter we're going to cover some of the typical scams that cyber-criminals will run in order to steal personal information or money, to help make sure you don't become a victim of fraud.

Social Engineering

Social engineering involves manipulating people and tricking them, taking advantage of psychology rather than using computer hacking, in order to get access or information.

Cyber-criminals sometimes target organizations with their social engineering attacks, looking for access to buildings, data or computer systems. When they attack individuals, it tends to be with the end-goal of getting passwords, bank information or the chance to install malware on your computer so that they can steal information that way.

You Can't Afford to Get Hacked

Using social engineering to get access to money and information is far easier than hacking into your software to get it, which is why there are so many scams of this nature out there.

It's a lot easier for a criminal to fool you into handing over your password, because you believe you're entering it into a legitimate site, than it is to guess or hack your account password. At least assuming you've followed our earlier advice on choosing a strong password!

A huge part of security is about knowing where to place your trust, and keeping your wits about you online. It's incredibly easy, using the anonymity of the internet, for a cyber-criminal to pretend to be somebody they're not. The same applies to websites; it's not a complicated thing to mock-up a version of a trusted website to attempt to trick somebody into submitting login information to a fake.

When somebody shows up at your house asking to check your water meter, it's a smart precaution to ask for some ID before you let them in. Apply the same common-sense approach to your online interactions.

So, how can you recognize a social engineering attack? Let's look at some of the places you might encounter them.

In An Email

When you receive an email from family, friends or work colleagues, chances are you open and trust it automatically. And fair enough, but maybe don't go clicking any links without closer inspection.

It's possible for hackers to get access to somebody's email address book, and use it to send out messages to all of the contacts within it, who will be more inclined to trust this message since it's coming from somebody they know.

So, pay attention to the little details. Is the message written in a way that the person normally writes? Are they asking you to do anything strange, or send information that you wouldn't expect them to need from you? Pay attention to those signs and, if you're suspicious, don't act on anything within the email before you can confirm with the sender that it's genuine.

There are a couple of things you should particularly watch out for:

Emails containing a link

The email might explain that you simply *have* to check out this link, teasing something interesting, useful or hilarious at the other end of it. If you do click on the link though, your computer might be infected with malware, letting the cyber-criminal take over your machine and carry on the cycle by sending the same email out to your whole address book.

Emails containing a download

Perhaps the download is of pictures, maybe it's a video or some music, or maybe it's disguised as an important document of some kind. Seeing that the email has come from a trusted contact, you might choose to download it… and the malicious software embedded in it. With access to your computer, and therefore your entire contact list, the criminal can spread the attack onwards.

> **Did you know?**
>
> 66% of malware is installed through deceptive email attachments, according to Verizon's 2018 Data Breach Investigations Report.

What about emails that don't come from people you know? We've all received the emails from princes, promising untold riches. Or successful businessmen on their deathbeds, who want us to distribute their fortunes to charities and keep a little for ourselves. Not to mention the wildly attractive women, who want to send us money and come to be with us!

These types of emails are called 'phishing emails'. They tell you a story that they hope will be compelling enough that you'll be prepared to send them personal information, such as bank account details, that they can use to steal from you.

They often come from backgrounds that look, at least at first glance, legitimate. Known institutions such as a company, bank or school that you're familiar with.

You'll find there are some common themes amongst phishing emails like these, here are a few patterns to watch out for:

Asking for urgent help

The email might claim that somebody you know and care about is stuck in another country, in trouble or in the hospital. They urgently need you to send some money so that they can get home, and if you reply they'll give you the details you need to send the funds to. Naturally, these will be the criminal's account details.

Asking for donations to a good cause

Manipulating your desire to support charitable causes, criminals send phishing emails asking for money to help with whatever natural disaster or charity is currently in the public consciousness.

Asking you to verify information

There may be a link in the email, and a request for you to follow that link and put in your login information. This might come with a warning that somebody has tried to access your account, and you need to verify your information to protect it (ironic, considering if you do verify your information, the hacker will have access to your account). The email may look legitimate, and the link may look like it goes to the right place, but this is a really common scam. These types of email will often play up the urgency of the scenario, because criminals know that the faster they can get you to act, the less time you'll have to think and possibly see through their scam.

Notifying you that you've won something

The email might claim that you've visited a site at exactly the right time, or that you've got an inheritance to collect, or even that you've won some kind of lottery. Of course, all you have to do to collect your winnings is hand over some personal information! They might need your bank details, so that your money can be sent over to your account, and possibly some personally identifying information so they can confirm who you are. Schemes like this rely on you wanting the prize so much that you don't think too hard about the legitimacy of the email.

Posing as a colleague or your boss

The scammer might pretend to be somebody you work with, asking for important work-related information, maybe something confidential. Alternatively, they might ask for information required to access company accounts, or payment details for a company credit card. As bad as it is to lose your own money or personal security, there's a whole other layer of risk involved if a scammer can get access to secure company information.

> **Did you know?**
> 22% of organizations see phishing as their greatest security threat, according to a 2018 EY Global Information Security Survey.

Scam Alert! Do Not Be the Victim of a Fraud

Phishing emails aren't always generic emails, sent to thousands of people at once. Sometimes they're specifically targeted to you, based on information a hacker has found out about you online, such as on your social media profiles. They approach you with a knowledge of you and your life that might seem shocking. These are dangerous, because with all of that information it becomes a lot easier for them to craft a story that you might find believable.

In the image below, we've got an example of the kind of email you might encounter in a phishing attack, with numbers to indicate particular areas to watch out for.

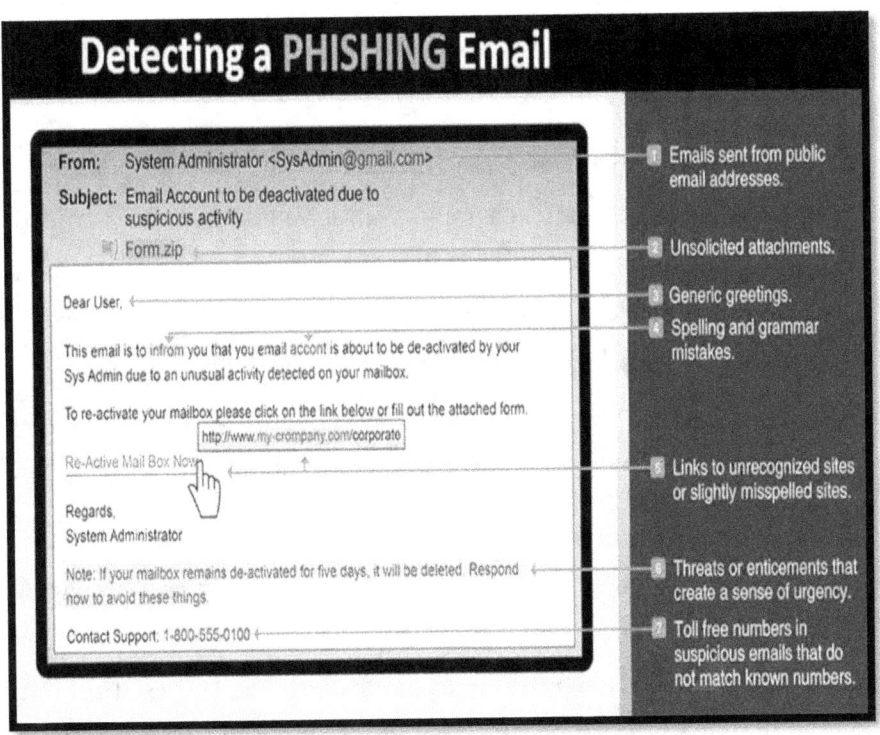

What happens after the email?

Hackers use phishing emails with a wide range of motivations, so if one does slip through the net and trip you up it's hard to say exactly what will happen next.

They may infect your system with malware, such as a virus that destroys all of your files or something that allows them to spy on whatever is happening on your system. The malware might encrypt all of your files, from personal photos to important work documents, and this might be followed up by a message from the criminal asking for ransom money before your files can be released.

This type of attack is called a 'ransomware' attack, and they're usually, although not exclusively, focused on organizations so they can ask for large amounts of money.

A particularly devastating example of ransomware was the 'Wannacry' ransomware that was unleashed in 2017, mostly targeting healthcare providers in Europe. This attack was a threat to more than just money or information, this went further and became a threat to people's health—even their lives. With all of their files inaccessible, doctors and nurses weren't able to access the information they needed to treat their patients, no matter how much they wanted to.

The ransomware also attacked computers that were managing hospital equipment and machinery, stopping them from functioning properly, and some patients died due to these problems within the health monitoring systems.

Scam Alert! Do Not Be the Victim of a Fraud

Wannacry ransomware was able to spread itself from a single device to all of the other devices connected to the same network, so it was able to spread incredibly quickly. The picture below illustrates the progress of the ransomware, and the way that every system that became encrypted would have a message pop up, asking for money in the form of the digital currency Bitcoin to be paid to the hacker to get proper computer access back.

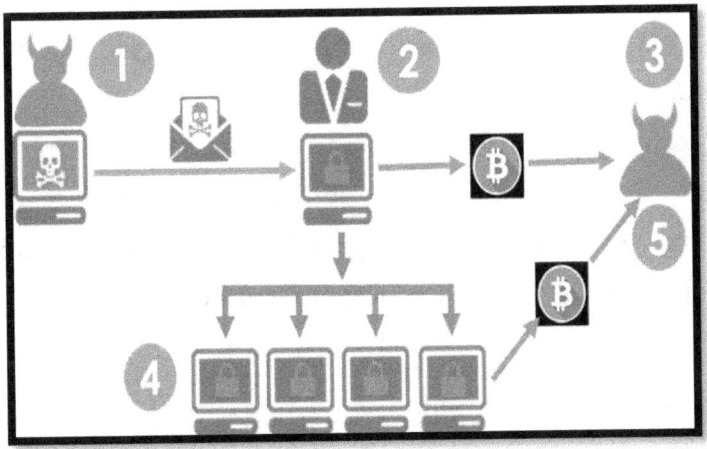

1. The ransomware virus is sent, for example in an email attachment.
2. The victim sees that their files have been encrypted, and that the only way to retrieve them is to send a Bitcoin payment to the cyber-criminal.
3. That victim sends their payment to release their files from the encryption, but this isn't the end of it…

4. Every other computer that was connected to the same network as the original victim's device has also been infected by the ransomware, and they all get the same messages.
5. Those people are forced to make Bitcoin payments to the hacker as well in order to have access to their computers and files again.

Should you pay the ransom money to get your access back?

If you are the victim of one of these scams, should you pay up? Unfortunately, the answer is not pleasant. It is not advised to pay the money. If you're wondering why, consider this question: is there any guarantee that you get your access back after payment is completed? If somebody is willing to design and carry out this kind of malicious attack, can you trust them to give your files back when they've been paid?

Ultimately, it is up to the circumstances and individuals and businesses to take whatever action they think is best, but the official advice is to treat those files as irretrievable and not pay the hacker.

In A Phone Call

A phishing scam that is only carried out over the phone is sometimes referred to as 'vishing'. The victim will get a call, usually on their private mobile phone, and possibly from a familiar number. The scammer in these instances may try to impersonate somebody you know, or might use a fake identity to attempt to fool you into handing over sensitive information or agreeing to send money to a specific account.

Criminals can use software packages to change the tone and apparent gender of their voices, as well as adding in background noises to the call to create a sense of urgency and encourage you to act without thinking.

As this kind of technology becomes cheaper and more readily available, these types of attacks are growing in popularity. In one 2019 incident, scammers used sophisticated voice faking technology to mimic the voice of a CEO, tricking a company manager into transferring $243,000 to the fraudster's account.

In A Text

There's been an increase in hackers making use of text messages for their scam attempts. The fraudster will send an unsolicited message with appealing offers, such as extremely low-interest personal loans, or a link to download free apps that you would normally have to pay for.

Sometimes these messages will attempt to scare you into replying or following any links they contain, for example by saying you're in violation of some tax code and need to provide certain information, or you will be investigated and possibly prosecuted.

Criminals often take advantage of current events, and there have been a number of malicious messages preying on people's fear of COVID-19, either stating that somebody you've been in contact with recently has been infected, and you should follow the link for more information, or falsely claiming that they have testing kits or vaccines for sale.

In a development of this kind of attack, recently some hackers have used WhatsApp messenger to find victims for a more involved scam. They first trick somebody into handing over a one-time code which they can use to install that person's WhatsApp on a different device. A hacker can then use that hijacked account to contact the friends and family of the original victim.

This can occur through other channels than WhatsApp, many different messaging services and social media platforms are vulnerable to the same manipulations.

Criminals have all sorts of ways of getting somebody to hand over the installation code that allows them to take control of a messaging account, most of which involve posing as a trusted friend or family member who is struggling to receive their own installation code.

People fall for this kind of scheme because they believe they're talking to somebody they know, and don't realize that the code they're receiving and passing over is actually *their own* code.

Once a hacker has been able to hijack an account, they might steal personal information from old messages or messages that continue to come in, they may ask for money in order to return access to the rightful owner, or they might go on to scam other people from the account holder's contact list.

In An Exciting Offer or Opportunity

Everybody loves the chance to get something for free! Of course, cyber-criminals are well aware of this, and they know that if they can offer something that sounds exciting enough, people will overlook their suspicions and do whatever they're asked to do in exchange for the prize.

They might offer a free download of a newly released movie or album, or of software that usually comes with a hefty price tag. In a slightly more subtle version, rather than giving something away for free the criminal may have set up an amazing deal on an auction site to lure in victims.

This type of scam can also be extended to physical space! Hackers sometimes leave USB drives lying around in public spaces, knowing that whoever finds it is likely to plug it in to take a look. Rather than some stranger's personal documents, that USB drive may come loaded with malware which, as soon as the device is connected to your computer, can infect and encrypt your files in the background.

Obviously, the results of these scams depend heavily on the method used to carry them out. Everything from losing money on an item that is never received, to having to pay a ransom to have files released, or even having financial information stolen and bank accounts ransacked.

On Social Media

There are a massive range of ways that hackers use social media to execute scams. When everything online can be fake—from the news, to the people sharing it—it's hard to know who and what to trust.

A lot of people are willing to share stories on social media based on nothing more than a quick look at the headline, and criminals can take advantage of this by spreading stories that are blown out of proportion, or just plain incorrect, in order to spread misinformation and encourage people to act in ways that make them more vulnerable to scammers.

These kinds of attacks can also be more personal; for example, you might receive a message from somebody you know claiming they've got pictures of you drunk, or in a compromising position. Click this link to check them out! And, of course, the temptation to have a look is huge—either because you know it can't be you, and you want to confirm, or you're worried it might be and want to see how bad those pictures are!

That link takes you to a login page for your Twitter, Instagram or Facebook account. Or that's what it looks like, at any rate. But chances are the pages is actually fake, and when you enter your login information it goes straight to the hacker, giving them complete access to and control over your social media account.

Don't Fall For Their Tricks!

Phishing attacks like the ones outlined so far are all over the place now, and hackers only need a few users to fall for them to consider their attack a success. But you don't have to be one of those people!

There are a few simple things you can do to make yourself significantly less likely to fall victim to these kinds of scams, and most of them fundamentally come down to paying more attention and thinking twice before taking action you're asked to take in some random message.

If you receive a suspicious message…

Slow down

Cyber-criminals rely on creating a false sense of urgency to persuade you to act first and ask questions later. Click this link, send this information, log in here in the next five minutes or you'll lose this opportunity!

If you receive a message with this kind of high-pressure messaging, don't let it sway you. Read the message carefully, consider where it's come from and verify any information elsewhere before acting on it.

Fact checks

People can say anything in a text message or email, and it isn't all that difficult for a hacker to make it look like a message has come from a company you know and might even use.

Be wary of any messages that supposedly come from respected companies; inspect the email address (you'll often find that, upon closer inspection, the email has come from somebody's personal gmail or hotmail account rather than an official company one), use a search engine to confirm the company's actual email address or phone number before you trust that the message has come from them.

Don't automatically trust links

You can hover over a link in an email to see the address that link will send you to at the bottom of your screen, which is a good first step to take before clicking on anything you're sent. Even so, a careful fake might lead you astray anyway. To be on the safe side, find the website independently by going through a search engine, so that you know you're going where you intend to go.

Don't trust downloads

Downloading a file can open you up to any number of attacks if it isn't entirely secure, so unless you know the sender personally, *and* you are expecting a specific file from them, never download anything in an email attachment. You can also get your antivirus to scan any email attachments before you download them, to provide an added level of security even when you trust the sender and know what you're expecting to receive.

The second part of this is absolutely vital. Cyber-criminals often get access to individual's email accounts, or other messaging accounts, as the first stage of any scam, so that they can send out their fake emails to a whole address book.

Just because a message seems to have come from somebody you know and trust, that doesn't guarantee that the message and its contents are legitimate and safe. If you get an email from a friend with an attachment that you weren't expecting, check with them via some other method of communication before you follow any links or download any files.

Ignore foreign offers

Any email claiming that you've won a foreign lottery, asking for your account information so they can transfer funds from a foreign country, or letting you know that a relative you've never heard of has left you money in their will are scams 100% of the time. These emails should be deleted promptly.

Additional ways to protect yourself

Those are all safety checks you should do whenever you receive a strange message—or even a message that looks totally normal! Social engineering and phishing attacks rely on human psychology to work, so there's only so much you can do on the technological side of things to keep yourself safe, but there are some protective measures you can put in place.

Immediately delete any requests for information

If a message asks you to reply with financial information, personal information or passwords, it's a scam. No reputable company will get in touch with you to ask for that information. Just delete it right away.

Reject unsolicited offers

Reputable organizations will not get in touch with you, out of the blue, to offer help with fixing up your credit score, getting better rates on loans, answering questions that you didn't ask, or anything else.

Unless you have made a specific request, treat any emails offering this kind of help as a scam and ignore/delete accordingly.

On a similar note, companies emailing you out of nowhere to ask *you* for help should be treated as suspicious.

If an email makes you want to offer help to a charity or organization you don't have a pre-existing relationship with, do some research online to be sure the organization is legitimate (websites like Charity Navigator, CharityWatch, GuideStar and the Charity Register for England and Wales can help you) and make any donations through official channels rather than by following an email link.

Make full use of spam filters

Whichever email program you use, you'll have a spam filter. You can check out your spam filter options in your email settings, and make sure they're set to high. If you're not sure how to do this, you'll be able to find a step-by-step guide by doing an internet search for 'spam filters' plus the name of the email program that you use.

It's a good idea to make a habit of regularly checking your spam folder, because legitimate emails do sometimes get caught out by them, but this will significantly reduce the number of phishing attempts you have to wade through on a daily basis!

Ensure your devices are secure

The same things that protect you from other cyber-threats apply here as well: make sure you have solid anti-virus software installed, that your firewalls are active and your email filters are in use and kept up to date.

Make sure you allow your operating system to apply any new updates and, for any devices or software that don't automatically update, regularly check for any available updates and apply them promptly.

Some Final Thoughts

Social engineering scams rely on taking advantage of human psychology. It's what makes them so difficult to counter at the technological level, but it also puts a lot of the power with you for avoiding them. If you find that a message you've received from a company or an unknown source makes you feel rushed or emotional, take a moment to consider why that is and whether this might be somebody trying to trick you into acting without thinking.

You Can't Afford to Get Hacked

You have the power to avoid phishing scams and social engineering attacks; have faith in yourself, and consider all incoming messages with a logical, unemotional approach. You'll be a cyber-criminal's worst nightmare!

Tech-Savvy Kids

Finally, let's talk about how to keep kids safe online. You can't protect somebody else if you don't understand how to protect yourself, which is why it was important to get a solid grounding in cybersecurity for your own devices and activities before we got here.

You can't teach what you don't know, but now that you've learned how to protect yourself in previous chapters, we can talk about how to protect your tech-savvy kids.

Being a parent can be both incredibly rewarding and desperately stressful. Giving a kid a tablet or smartphone can be an easy way to keep them occupied and entertained, and can even have educational purposes. And if it's sometimes to grab a precious minute of peace and quiet in the car for the sake of your sanity, that's not unusual either!

It's normally a safe and harmless way for your kid to spend a few minutes, but there can be downsides over the long term—lack of focus, and increased symptoms of anxiety and depression, for example.

This chapter isn't going to look at those downsides, and we're not going to discuss rules for parents about how old kids should be before they own phones, or how to set boundaries around screens at the dinner table. Parenting advice is not our area of expertise, and it's beyond the scope of this book.

What we are going to do is to highlight the fact that your kids are as vulnerable as you are to cyber-crime, along with a whole host of other online dangers.

Children can access inappropriate or adult content—by accident, or intentionally. Use of social media can open them up to cyberbullying, or lead them to get involved in bullying somebody else online.

Media online can cause kids to form unrealistic expectations of how they should look, or the way their lives should go, and they can succumb to the pressure to overshare details of their lives. The internet can promote dangerous behaviors, like meeting strangers they've encountered online, and there's the truly terrifying risk of sexual predators grooming kids.

We're going to go through some of the major risks that kids face online, specifically risks that threaten young people disproportionately, and some things that you can put in place to protect your kids and keep them safe.

Cyberbullying

Once upon a time, when the bell rang for the end of the school day that meant an end to bullying. Not anymore. Now that millions of children use computers or phones every day, there's no easy escape from bullies or dysfunctional social relationships. Cyberbullying is a growing problem, with almost double the number of school children experiencing cyberbullying in 2019 compared to 2007[5].

Cyberbullying can involve sending insults, hateful messages or even death threats. It can include spreading lies about the victim through social media and leaving nasty comments that are publicly visible on their social media profiles. Sometimes cyberbullying gets more involved, with the bully (or bullies) setting up fake profiles or web pages to make cruel comments, spread rumors and generally harass the victim.

Even if the account is reported and deleted, the nature of the internet means that these things can already have been shared far and wide.

In-person bullying might be a single event, or a string of connected events, but cyberbullying has a whole different kind of reach. Cyberbullying can follow the victim around, wherever they go, and the impact can spread long after the initial contact.

---

[5] 18.8% of children surveyed had experienced cyberbullying in 2007, compared to 36.5% in 2019, according to a study by the Cyberbullying Research Center.

Kids might well try to hide the fact that they're being cyberbullied from their parents. They might be afraid of a parental overreaction, or worried that they won't be allowed to use the internet at home if their parents find out.

> **Did you know?**
>
> 87% of young people have witnessed cyberbullying happening online, according to McAfee's 2014 Teens and Screens study.

Internet safety tips

- Bullying is typically related to school life, and your kid will understand the full situation far better than you do. Make it a priority to listen to them and understand their perspective before you take action, as it will be helpful in getting to the bottom of things.
- If your child is being bullied through instant messaging, help them to use the 'block' or 'ban' feature so that the bully can no longer contact them.
- If harassing emails are an ongoing problem, you can help your child to delete that email account and set up a new one. Talk to them about the importance of only giving that address to family members and trusted friends.

- Encourage your child not to respond to bullying messages or posts on social media. Keep a record of the emails and other instances of bullying as proof. If the bullying continues, or begins to escalate, contact the police.
- If your child is younger, and does not have their own device (meaning they are carrying out online activity through your computer or tablet), you can insist that all online activity is supervised so that you can support them if bullying messages or posts come through.

Sexual Predators

Around 1 in 7 kids have been sexually solicited online[6]. 25% of children have been exposed to unwanted pornographic material while using the internet, and 20% of teenagers who regularly go online say they have had an unwanted sexual solicitation through the internet[7].

Those are awful statistics, but it's important to understand the scope of the problem.

Sexual predators often target young people in chat rooms, then moving the conversation over to social networking sites where there is more information. Predators often take on fake identities and pretend to have an interest in the young person's favorite music, movies or hobbies.

---

[6] According to John Shehan, CyberTipline program manager for the National Center for Missing and Exploited Children (Alexandria, Virginia).
[7] Statistics from the Crimes Against Children Research Center.

Predators often attempt to manipulate young people into participating in a criminal sexual relationship by appealing to their desire to be understood and appreciated, and by playing into the excitement of taking risks.

Internet safety tips

- Tell your kids to be careful how much personal information they put online. They should avoid posting their full name, phone number, address—or other information that could give away their physical location. Things like the name of their school, or photos of them in a team sweatshirt, can provide clues about where they live that could put them at risk.
- Talk to your kids about not sending photos to people they meet online. For younger children you might leave the conversation there, for children aged 12 and upwards though it's important to emphasize the risks of sending sexual pictures. Make it very clear to teenagers that sending sexual pictures of themselves or other kids their age can constitute child pornography, and producing or sending those pictures is a serious crime.
- Put your computer in a common area of your home so that you can keep an eye on their online activities. This obviously applies more easily to children who don't yet have their own phone with internet access, or their own laptop or tablet. You can find websites that will explain the acronyms young people are using in instant messaging (things like 'LMIRL' =

'let's meet in real life', or 'POS' = 'parent over shoulder') so that you know what's happening.
- Have conversations with your kids about the online friendships they have, and encourage them to report anything that makes them uncomfortable to you or another trusted adult as soon as it happens. Make sure they know that you want them to feel safe, and that it isn't their fault if somebody asks them for information they don't want to share, or tries to get them to do something inappropriate.

Pornography

Many parents are understandably worried about pornography popping up online to surprise their children. What a lot of parents don't realize though is that some kids go online to deliberately look for this kind of material.

You can check the internet browser history to get a look at which websites your children are visiting, but a lot of kids are aware of this and able to delete this history.

To make sure they're protected from seeing inappropriate images or videos, you may want to install some filtering software to block porn sites on your home network.

Internet safety tips

- Install filtering software to block porn sites on any computer your child has access to. Sometimes you can do this through your router, and you can do an internet search for 'how to

block sites on [your router]' to find guides to doing this; this provides an added measure of protection if your kids are older and using mobile devices to browse the internet without the opportunity for you to supervise.
- You may also want to consider installing software to monitor and record conversations that occur over instant messaging, or in chat rooms, as well as websites visited.
- It can be helpful to have conversations with your kids from a young age to make it clear that they can ask you anything that they're curious about, so that they might come to you before asking a search engine and potentially finding images that they aren't ready to see.

Additional Technical Control Measures

We're going to look at some specific control measures that you can put in place on the technology in your house, to add some protection for your kids.

Internet routers

You can use your internet router settings to put blocks in place for specific websites, or set up adult content controls to prevent your kids from being able to access inappropriate websites.

Your router may also allow you to set schedules, to limit your kids' screen time. This is good for limiting the time that kids can spend online late at night, when you aren't able to keep an eye on things.

There are a lot of useful guides that you can find online by searching for 'Parental Control Routers', if you want to choose a router based which of these features it has.

Device-specific security

Smartphones and tablets with different operating systems can have controls put in place to make sure usage is age-appropriate. Kids often want to be able to participate in all different elements of online life, and the point at which they're old enough to have their own devices, but you still need to have some control over their internet usage, can be a tricky period of time to manage.

Online communication is not only a core way for young people to maintain their friendships these days, it's also increasingly becoming integral to their education, as more schools are using online resources and tasks as part of the curriculum.

For all of the good that the internet can do though, it can also open up the potential for peer pressure, cyberbullying or dangerous interactions with strangers.

Parents need to make their own decisions about when is the best time for their kids to have their own devices, be it a smartphone, tablet or laptop. And for younger children, there are some useful controls you can put in place to manage their device usage and keep them safe.

Locking up screen time

It's quite straightforward to put limits on how often you child has access to their device. You can do this simply by setting up a passcode, lock screen pattern or fingerprint recognition, so the device can only be used under your supervision.

This security function should be implemented anyway, as a protective measure in case the phone is lost or stolen.

This can be done on Apple devices through the 'Touch ID & Passcode' section of the phone's settings, and on an Android device by going into the settings and then to 'Security & Location' or 'Security'.

Apps

When your kids first have their own devices, make sure only age-appropriate apps are downloaded onto them. It's also a good idea to make sure your child can't use those apps to make in-app purchases. Avoid this by making sure that you don't link your credit card or bank account to the app store.

In 2017, a father in Lancashire, UK, found out that his 11-year-old son had spent almost £6000 through apps over two weekends. That's around $7465.

The apps are designed to make these purchases as appealing as possible—and as seamless! So, make sure your kids can't be tempted by not having your cards linked up.

Monitoring services and parental control apps

You can download a monitoring app to your child's device so that you can see what's going on and keep an eye on things. Apple has a Screentime app that you can download specifically for mobile services, and you can set up parental controls for app downloads on Google Play.

The applications to introduce parental controls onto your children's devices and closely monitor activity are more suitable for really young children. These apps can constitute a violation of privacy for older children and teenagers, who need to be able to feel some autonomy.

For very young users though, they can be extremely helpful for keeping track of online activity.

Social Media

Social media websites such as Facebook, Instagram and Twitter are a massive part of life these days, and children will want to get involved. Probably earlier than you'd like them to! Whichever site they want to join, it's worth having a look around the system yourself first so that you can get a look at the privacy controls offered.

You can apply the various privacy measures for social media that we talked about in previous chapters, and here we're going to highlight a few additional tips you can use.

Before we dive in to specific sites, bear in mind that many of these have a minimum age for users. It isn't unusual for children to lie about their ages in order to set up accounts on social media websites; despite most platforms having a minimum age of 13, around half of children aged 11 to 12 have a social media profile[8].

---

[8] 46% of 11-year-olds and 51% of 12-year-olds, according to the Children and Parents Media Use and Attitudes report by Ofcom, 2017.

Facebook

If your child sets up a Facebook account, you might want to establish that you will have access to the account—not just as a 'friend', but by sharing the login details, so that you can see any notifications and messages that are sent and received.

Just as with the monitoring apps and parental controls that we discussed earlier, it's important to strike a balance between protecting your child and respecting their right to privacy.

Also, for children under 13, too young to have their own Facebook account, there is a Messenger Kids application which might make for a good compromise!

Twitter

There are a lot of privacy controls you can—and should—put in place on a Twitter account. Once it's set up, you can go for a tour of the 'Settings and Privacy' tab and make sure everything is set up for your kid the way you want it.

The 'Protect Your Tweets' option should be selected so that only accepted followers on the account are able to see your child's tweets and reply to them.

You should also disable the 'Location' setting, so that GPS and location-based information won't be available in tweets.

Under the 'Direct Messages' tab, there are a few settings to check. You can make sure direct messages from non-followers are disabled, so that your child can't be contacted by strangers, and there's also a 'Quality' message feature that you can enable to reduce spam messages.

'Discoverability' is a feature which links email addresses and phone numbers to a Twitter account, so that it becomes searchable by that information, and you should make sure that is disabled for your kids.

Finally, under 'Safety', you can choose to mask public content that is deemed sensitive. This can hide any images or content on Twitter that might be inappropriate or distressing.

Instagram

Being an image-based social media platform, it's even more important that your child's Instagram account is locked down to strangers. Their account should be set to 'Private', to ensure that anything they share is only visible to accepted followers, and can't be commented on by anybody they haven't approved.

You can find this under 'Settings', then 'Privacy', then 'Account Privacy'. It's also straightforward to block individual accounts by going to their profile, tapping the drop-down menu by their name to open it up and selecting 'Block/Unblock'.

Other platforms

There are a huge range of other social media platforms out there, and more developing all the time. We'll talk a little more about some specific platforms, but remember that you need to talk to your kids about any new sites they develop an interest in, and potentially do your own research to work out what measures need to be put in place.

Twitch

Twitch is officially designed for users older than 13, but it's very easy for younger children to access the platform and watch streams. A lot of gamers use Twitch to stream gaming sessions during which they can chat with their audience, and viewers can donate to their favorite streamers.

Public chats on Twitch are moderated, but with such a huge number of users it's inevitable that certain things will slip through the net. If your child likes to use Twitch, it's probably a good idea to spend some time watching with them so you can get a sense for who they're following and whether the conversations in the spaces they're following are mostly appropriate.

Snapchat

This platform has gained a lot of population recently, particularly with young people—although, as with many of these sites, you are supposed to be at least 13 years old to create an account. It's worth having a close look at the privacy settings on any account your kid sets up, to make sure location data isn't being shared and strangers aren't able to view the pictures they send.

Most popular games and services will have simple, step-by-step guides to privacy and security that you can find with a quick internet search, and we encourage you to read these.

YouTube Kids

Don't worry about Momo—focus your concerns on YouTube Kids

YouTube Kids has earned its own section, for reasons we'll explore in a moment, but first let's talk about Momo.

Momo is a character with bulging eyes, a sinister over-wide smile and stringy hair, which was rumored to appear on sites and apps such as YouTube, Facebook and WhatsApp. It would apparently appear to ask kids to complete tasks and challenges, some of them involving dangerous activities, self-harm or even suicide. There was much debate over whether Momo was real or not, with some people convinced it was a hoax and some insisting that their children had encountered Momo.

In the end, Momo turned out to be a viral hoax. And all of that well-intentioned concerned might have been better focused on the children's channels on YouTube, many of which are genuinely full of potentially distressing and dangerous content for children.

There have been a number of instances of videos on YouTube Kids with inappropriate content, including graphic violence or suicide advice, sandwiched between cartoon scenes as a kind of deeply sick joke.

An article by Wired in 2017 highlighted a few particularly worrying examples, including 'Paw Patrol' characters attempting suicide, inappropriate sexualisation of Disney princesses, videos of children apparently terrified, and disturbing cartoon violence.

This has been a long-term battle for YouTube, its main platform and the version supposedly curated for children.

The core difficulty that YouTube faces here is that it relies on a system of 'flagging' inappropriate content before it can be taken down. This, of course, means that somebody has to come across and see the video before anything can be done about it.

There's no system in place for pre-moderation, and people viewing videos in full before they can be approved and uploaded to YouTube Kids. This would be the only way to really keep the platform safe from pranksters and trolls, but the site has shown no indication that it will take a step like this. YouTube frequently highlights what it calls its 'robust' content-reporting features when content controversies arise, but the disturbing videos keep coming nonetheless.

When you download the YouTube Kids app you'll find a disclaimer from the developer to explain the situation; 'We work hard to offer a safer YouTube experience, but no automated system is perfect.' You don't say? The honest truth is that YouTube was never designed with a younger audience in mind. So far, it doesn't seem likely to be able to step up and protect the kids who are watching.

Even when the problematic content isn't that extreme, there are issues that can arise through unsupervised YouTube viewing.

You Can't Afford to Get Hacked

If you leave a train-obsessed five-year-old with an iPad, watching videos of trains pulling into stations, for just a few minutes, you risk returning to videos of train accidents. There are channels on YouTube that appear totally innocent on the surface, but which are actually full of right-wing propaganda, aiming to radicalize young people who are still forming their ideas about the world.

YouTube celebrities are not always the best influences either. There's always some new controversy, some more worrying than others, and all likely to lead to depressing conversations with your kids about the latest antics.

From YouTubers casually using racial slurs on their live streams, to Twitch streamers who casually tell people in the comments to kill themselves, these are not people you necessarily want your children to be following or emulating.

In fairness, the majority of the content on YouTube Kids is neither distressing nor disturbing. Most of it is just rubbish. An overwhelming majority of the videos uploaded to 'kid-friendly' YouTube are terrible, purely designed to cater to the algorithm. Nonsense songs and stories with images or toys of popular characters to draw views, but nothing of substance.

The aim of these is not to provide genuine entertainment, or educate children, it's just to grab and keep kids' attention. Toddlers, for all their great qualities, do not have great critical faculties! They're happy to watch nursery rhyme videos with poor production values and endless repetition for hours on end.

What can you do about it?

As a parent, only you can decide on the best way to handle kids and YouTube. We don't make any claims as to one 'best' way to deal with the situation, but we have some suggestions.

The most straightforward solution, particularly with young children, may be to get rid of YouTube from all of the devices in your home. It can be a bit of a project, but it's the safest way to ensure your children don't stumble across something you don't want them to see.

It isn't unreasonable to be concerned—or even just irritated!—by YouTube Kids, and there are plenty of places where you can find much higher-quality video entertainment for children, such as Netflix or BBC iPlayer, or reputable advert-free games designed for young players.

If you still want to have access to YouTube, and allow your children to watch it, it might be wise to only allow them to watch it under direct supervision. If you're sat with them, you can steer them away from recommendations that point towards inappropriate content, and close down any videos that take a dangerous turn.

Additional Advice

Shared computers

A lot of children use family computers, and don't have their own devices. It's easy to assume that children, not having their own credit cards, aren't at risk for financial crime online. But, while sharing a device with parents, their activity can potentially affect other users. And vice versa; kids can check the browser history on a computer and be exposed to sites that their parents have visited previously.

If parents and children are sharing a computer, there should be separate user accounts. That way the children don't have access to their parents' files and browser data.

Identity theft

You might be surprised to know that children's IDs are incredibly valuable to criminals. Kids are ideal targets for identity theft, because they have perfect credit scores—so a criminal can take out credit in their name—and often don't find out that their identity has been compromised until years later, when they go to take out loans or apply for their own credit cards.

Teach your children to protect themselves from this risk by limiting the information they share about themselves as much as possible.

Passwords

Make sure your kids understand the importance of not sharing their passwords, even with close friends, and also of logging out of accounts when they've finished using them. Particularly when they're using shared computers, such as those found in school or libraries.

And a message to the parents

Strictly speaking, this isn't really cybersecurity, but it's important all the same. As a parent, please do not post revealing photos of your children on social media accounts. Photos of babies in the bath, or toddlers playing naked around the house, are very cute memories to have! But they shouldn't be shared online.

For one thing, we're all aware now that images on the internet are around forever, and it isn't fair to your kids in the future to put these pictures of them up when they can't consent to it. It's a violation of their privacy, fundamentally, and when they grow up it should be their choice how much of their life is visible online.

Secondly, and more worryingly, you can never be completely sure where those pictures will end up.

There have been known instances of private Facebook groups where people share pictures of other people's children and make fun of them. That's obviously nasty, but not necessarily harmful.

Worse than that though, is the risk of a child predator seeing those pictures and downloading them. Especially if they go on to put together information shared on your social media profiles, about where you live, where your kids go to school, and so on.

The only way to guarantee that your children's images are private is to *keep* them private, and not share them on the internet.

We absolutely do not intend to give parenting advice, that isn't our aim with this book. We are not aiming to tell people how to raise their children. All we want to do is give you a grounding in some of the risks children face online, things that you might not have been aware of in the past, and arm you with the tools you need to keep your families safe as they navigate the internet.

Now You're Ready!

Throughout this book we've talked about a number of risks that you might be facing online on a day-to-day basis. We've explained some of the ways that cyber-criminals seek to get hold of and use your information, and we've provided you with tips and tools to protect yourself and your family while using the internet.

We hope you've found this useful, and that you can start to put into practice the ideas we've given you to explore the internet with confidence and make life that much harder for the hackers.

Stay safe!

About the Authors

Amjad Pirotti is a project management professional and a ScrumMaster with over 16 years of cross-industry experience. Having led academies and R&D departments, he has been actively involved in training, teaching and research, and published in reputable journals. He has recently developed two master's degree programs, M.Sc. FinTech: Blockchain & Digital Currencies, and M.Sc. Internet of Things & Advanced Interaction, for two European universities.

Amir Roknifard is the founder of Academician journal and has reviewed few books in cybersecurity with more than 16 years of professional experience in cybersecurity. Over the years he has focused on cybersecurity services with a broader attitude of threat and vulnerability management, to reform cybersecurity process and procedure, helping boards to identify their risks and transform their cybersecurity practices. He has recently developed a master's degree program, M.Sc. Cybersecurity & Digital Forensics, for a European university.

www.ingramcontent.com/pod-product-compliance
Lightning Source LLC
Chambersburg PA
CBHW070242220526
45465CB00004B/1485